Timeless Whispers

A Heartfelt Gratitude

Charu Nagpal

BookLeaf Publishing

India | USA | UK

Dedication

To the Universe,

*For illuminating my path in this journey of
self-discovery and gratitude.*

*To those who have stood by me, in love and
spirit,*

Your unwavering support has been my strength.

To all the souls seeking the light within,

May this book serve as a beacon of hope,

A gentle reminder that we are all connected,

*And a testament that through gratitude, we
uncover our true selves.*

Acknowledgement

This book is the culmination of countless moments of reflection, inspiration, and the unwavering support. As I pen these acknowledgements, my heart is brimming with gratitude for everyone who has been a part of this journey.

To my daughter, my fur felines, my brother and my besties, your constant encouragement and belief in my dreams have been my guiding light. Your understanding, patience, and love have given me the strength to bring these words to life.

To my parents and my husband, thank you for your invaluable guidance and feedback, and for sharing your wisdom with me. Your insights and encouragement have shaped my voice and helped me refine each time I felt the lag.

To my readers, your curiosity and enthusiasm for poetry inspire me every day. Your support means the world to me, and I am honored to share these poems with you.

To the universe, for whispering timeless wisdom into my heart and reminding me that gratitude is the powerful force that binds us all.

And finally, to the quiet moments of solitude that allowed me to listen deeply to the whispers of my soul—thank you for providing the space where these poems could be born.

Preface

In a world where time rushes by, carrying us along in its relentless current, we often forget to pause and truly listen. Yet, in those rare, quiet moments— when we stop to breathe— we can hear the whispers of our hearts: timeless, gentle reminders of the beauty that surrounds us and the gratitude we owe to the universe.

"Timeless Whispers" is a collection born from these moments of stillness, a series of poetic reflections on the transformative power of gratitude. Each poem is a testament to the strength found in cherishing life's simple joys, the grace in embracing our struggles, and the profound peace that gratitude brings to our souls.

This book is more than just a compilation of words; it is a journey—a journey through the heart's most intimate corridors, where gratitude flows like a life-giving river, nourishing every part of our being. These poems are whispers of an eternal truth: that gratitude transforms our perspective, heals our wounds, and elevates our spirits.

As you turn these pages, may you hear the whispers of your own heart resonating with mine. May you be reminded of the countless blessings that fill your life, and find inspiration to embrace each day with a heart brimming with thankfulness.

With heartfelt gratitude,
Charu

To The Little Things

In quiet fields where daisies grow,
The morning dew, a tender glow,
A robin's song at break of day,
These little things, in a quiet sway.

The humble bee on petals bright,
The moon that softly lights the night,
The whispering leaves, the gentle breeze,
The symphony of the rustling trees.

A brook that dances over stones,
The fragrant blooms where wind has blown,
The sunlight's kiss upon my face,
Nature's tender, warm embrace.

The simple joys, the quiet grace,
Of nature's gentle, loving space,
In every leaf and bloom and stream,
Life's beauty shines in a radiant dream.

So here I stand, with heart so full,
In nature's lap, so bountiful,
Grateful for each simple thing,
The silent gifts the seasons bring.

Nurturing Moments Of Bliss

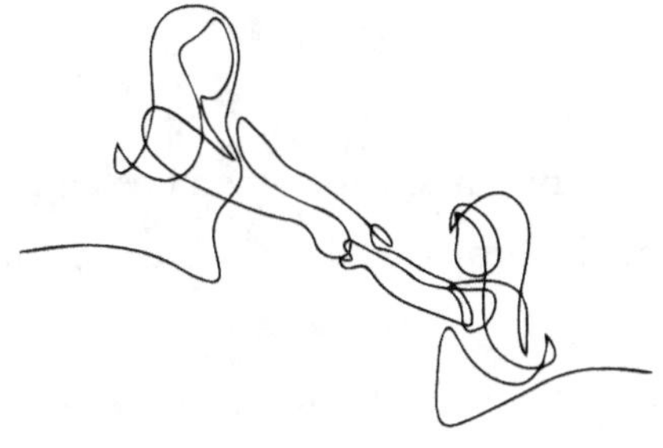

In the hush of twilight's grace, I hold you
near,
With each tender sip, my heart knows bliss.
Grateful am I for this sacred bond we share,
In these moments, love's purest kiss.

Cradling my precious one, I witness the soft
motion of her eyes.
The gentle rise and fall of a tiny chest.
Dainty hands curl around my finger,
Breaths mingling in the stillness,
And in this intimate embrace, the world
outside fades.

The warmth of love, an unseen grace,
Fills the space where words fall short.
Each sigh, each delicate movement,
A testament to the tender connection we
share.

In these moments, time stretches and bends,
Offering a glimpse of eternity in the fleeting
present.
Each time we lie together, skin to skin, heart
to heart,
Beholden whispers its true voice softly.
For in the simple act of closeness, in the silent
exchange of presence,
I experience a joy that defies description.

In these moments, my world is complete,
Held within the tender embrace of my baby.

Unfading Inner Child

An old man stands at ninety-nine,
With twinkling eyes and heart divine,
A playful soul, unbound by age,
A life lived fully, page by page.

With steps still light, though years have
passed,
He finds the present unsurpassed,
In moments small, he finds delight,
In morning's glow and stars at night.

With every breath, a gift he sees,
In whispered winds and rustling trees.
In every breeze and bird's soft song,
He feels a youth that's ever strong.

Not worried for the coming dawn,
But thankful for each breath drawn.
At twilight years, with hair like snow,
He dances still, though steps so slow.

But in his heart, the youth remains,
Unfettered by life's aches and pains.
In each moment spent on earth,
He finds pleasure, profound in mirth.

With gratitude, his heart does swell,
In every joy and story to tell.

Fervent Reverence

In the quiet corners of my heart,
I find echoes of a life I once knew,
A time when my world was simple,
Bound by the comforting walls of my
mother's home.

The space where I felt unburdened,
Where every corner whispered familiarity,
And each day unfolded with ease,
Now seems like a distant dream,
A past that slips through my fingers.

I carry with me the weight of new
responsibilities,
The financial strains and the emotional
distance,
A stark contrast to the carefree days of youth,
When my worries were few and my joys were
many.

I see my parents growing older,
Their faces lined with time and concern,
And my heart aches with a bittersweet
gratitude,
For the love they continue to offer,
Even as I am miles away from the home I once
took for granted.

In my new life, I grapple with a yearning,
A longing for the freedom of my past self,
For the simplicity of being,
Unshackled by the complexities of adulthood.
Yet, amidst this whirlwind of change,
I hold close the essence of what I have
learned,

The value of the home I grew up in,
And the enduring presence of those who
shaped me.
Gratitude fills my heart for the path I now
tread,
For the lessons learned and the love still felt,
Even as I navigate this new chapter,
A part of me will always remain tethered
To the cherished memories of the life I left
behind.

Fading Resonance

Once, our bond flowed like a waterfall,
Unspoken words danced between us,
A language only we understood,
In laughter and silence, our hearts spoke.

You knew my thoughts before I spoke them,
Our eyes exchanged secrets, no words needed,
I'd see the mischief in your gaze,
And in my smile, you'd find your answer.

We shared moments both sweet and wild,
Our days a tapestry of shared glances,
Now, our paths have diverged,
Yet, in memory, our friendship glistens.

Like a river that starts with a roar,
Our connection flowed with vibrant force,
Over time, it settled into gentle currents,
Carrying us to different shores.

We are no longer side by side,
But in the landscape of each other's minds,
We remain vibrant echoes,
Even as we drift through busy lives.
You are a cherished refrain in my heart,
A melody that hums softly in the background,
Our bond, though distant, remains a sweet
memory,
An eternal dance of understanding and joy.

Divine Trust

From the first breath in the cradle's embrace,
To the final sigh in the twilight's grace,
Life unfolds in mysterious ways,
A path unknown, through nights and days.

Helpless, we enter this world so vast,
Our fate like leaves in autumn's blast,
Guided by hands unseen, divine,
We trust in the sacred, the grand design.

Through trials and joys, we stumble and rise,
Seeking answers in the boundless skies,
Our hearts, though weary, find solace still,
In the quiet whisper of a higher will.

In youth, we dream with fervent desire,
Eyes alight with an inner fire,
Yet life's tempest can cast us down,
Leaving us lost, with hopes that drown.

But in surrender, we find our peace,
A silent prayer, our fears release,
For in the hands of the divine, we see,
A purpose beyond what our eyes decree.

As time weaves its tapestry, thin and wide,
We learn to flow with the eternal tide,
Helplessness becomes a sacred trust,
In the cosmic dance, from dust to dust.

In the twilight of life, as shadows fall,
We feel the pull of the celestial call,
Leaving all burdens at the divine's feet,
In the final embrace, our soul's retreat.

From birth's first cry to death's last breath,
We walk the path, through life and death,
In helplessness, we find our way,
Leaving all to God, day by day.

Unseen Hearts

In the quiet ache of night,
I yearn for your voice,
The tender words that once warmed me,
Now echoes of silence fall.

You, the love of my life,
Seem distant, indifferent,
Your absence a void that swallows my hope,
A painful reminder of what was once
cherished.

Yet, amidst this longing,
A steadfast friend stands by,
Through every storm and trial,
His presence a constant, though often
unnoticed.

He is the unsung hero,
Offering solace in my darkest hours,
His love a quiet strength,
Yet, my eyes remain turned elsewhere.

I have taken him for granted,
His patience a silent sacrifice,
In the corner of my heart,
A flicker of gratitude struggles to be seen.

The love I seek from you is elusive,
While his unwavering support is
overshadowed,
I recognize the gift of his loyalty,
Yet I remain blind to the depths of his
devotion.
In the corner of my heart,
A suppressed gratitude persists,
For the lives we lead, intertwined,
And the silent battles fought by those who
care.

Though my heart aches for your affection,
I must acknowledge the quiet strength beside
me,
A gratitude buried under layers of longing,
For the love that stands firm, though
unspoken.

A Sigh Of Silent Strength

As the world around her sleeps, she sits alone,
A tender life beside her, fragile, innocent,
She gazes upon her child, her daughter,
A blessing she knows, yet fear grips her heart,
For in the eyes of others, she sees the
shadows,
The silent judgments, the unspoken disdain.

She knows the whispers will come,
The cold glances, the tightening of lips,
She feels the weight of expectation,
The burden of tradition, the chains of the
past,

Her heart pounds with the fear of rejection,
For she has not given a son, an heir,
But a daughter, a gift from the gods.

In her soul, a storm rages,
A battle between love and fear,
She wishes to shield her child,
To protect her from the cruelty of the world,
Yet she knows the path ahead is steep,
Lined with thorns and brambles,
For in the eyes of those who should cherish,
She fears only the sting of disappointment.

But as she holds her daughter close,
She feels a strength within, ancient, eternal,
A voice whispers to her, soft yet strong,
"Fear not, for this child is a warrior,
A beacon of light in the darkness,
She carries within her the fire of the
goddesses,
And none shall dim her light."

She wipes away her tears,
Resolves to stand tall, unyielding,
For she knows her daughter's worth,
Is beyond measure, beyond the grasp of small
minds,
And she will fight, with the fury of a lioness,
To ensure her daughter walks in the sun,
Proud and free, unchained by the past,
For she is not just a daughter,
She is a queen in the making,
Destined to rise, to rule, to shine.

Fur And Faith

In the early hours, when the world is still,
She rises with weary eyes and a heavy heart,
The demands of the day lie before her,
endless,
Yet her spirit does not falter,
For she is a mother, a warrior of love.
Her days are long, filled with tasks unceasing,
At the office, she wears a mask of strength,
Balancing deadlines and duties,

But her mind is never far from home,
Where a tiny heart beats, waiting for her
return.
When she steps through the door,
Exhaustion clings to her like a shadow,
But there's no rest, not yet,

For her little one calls, with a cry, with a
need,
And she answers, as she always does,
With a touch, with a smile, with a lullaby.

And then, in the quiet corners of her home,
They come to her aid, silent and soft,
Her feline companions, with eyes of wisdom,
They circle the baby, gentle and watchful,
A purr here, a nuzzle there,
A love that needs no words, no explanations.
In their presence, she finds a moment's peace,

A quiet comfort, a shared understanding.
They care for the child in ways only they can,
A bond of trust, of warmth, of silent
affection,
And in those moments, she breathes easier,
Knowing she is not alone in this journey.
As night falls, she lies down,
Her mind heavy, yet her heart light.
For she knows, in the deepest part of her,
That love speaks in many tongues,

And sometimes, the most profound love,
Is the one that needs no voice,
But is felt in the soft brush of fur,
In the silent vigil of watchful eyes,
And in the gentle purrs that soothe her to
sleep.

A Mother's Heart: Dancing Through Rain and Time

In the soft rain's embrace,
A figure twirls with a grace that mirrors my
past,
Each drop that falls echoes the rhythm of
forgotten days.
Her laughter, a symphony that sings of
youthful dreams,
And as she dances,
I see my own reflection.

A shadow of a time when the world was a vast
playground,
And every rainstorm was a festival of joy.

Her steps are unburdened,
A dance of pure, unrestrained delight,
A reflection of my own heart's exuberance
from years gone by.

In her eyes, I find the same spark,
The same wonder that once lit up my
childhood,
A mirror of my essence,
Carried forth through the endless cycle of
time.
The rain falls gently around her,
Each drop a declaration to the beauty of her
spirit,
A celebration of life's simple pleasures.

And I stand here, overwhelmed,
In the quiet of this moment,
Feeling a profound connection,
Not just to her, but to a part of myself I
thought I had lost.
This is not merely a dance;
It is a reunion of souls.

A joyous reminder that within her,
Lives the vibrant echoes of my own youth.
And in her happiness, I find a reflection of
my own,
A bond that transcends the boundaries of
time and space,
A dance of love, eternal and ever true.

In The Shadows Of Love

In the home where shadows play,
Where manipulation clouds the day,
I find myself caught in their game,
Yet it's my husband's love that keeps me the
same.

Their words are daggers, sharp and cold,
A story of power that's silently told.
With every smile, a hidden snare,
I walk this path with a heart laid bare.

My dreams are tangled in their schemes,
Lost in the web of fractured dreams.
Yet, in the silence, where my heart screams,
His love is the light that redeems.

I stay for him, though the nights are long,
In a house where the right feels wrong.
My spirit bruised, but still I cling,
To the love that makes my heart sing.

Caught between duty and the need to be free,
I wrestle with shadows that no one else can
see.
Yet in his eyes, a gentle plea,
Keeps me bound, though my heart yearns to
flee.

Rising Resilience

In the heart of struggle, where darkness play,
And life's harsh winds blow us astray,
Resilience blooms in the cracks of despair,
A testament to the strength we declare.

Amidst the tempest and the torrid fight,
When dreams seem distant, lost from sight,
We find a spark that lights the way,
A beacon through the longest day.

Through shattered hopes and battles fought,
In the silence where battles are wrought,
We gather courage, piece by piece,
Building strength from pain's release.

Growth emerges from the deepest strife,
A lesson learned, a renewed life.
Each scar a story, each tear a guide,
Leading us to the strength inside.

In the face of hardship, we rise anew,
Forged by trials, our spirits true.
We are not defined by the storms we face,
But by the grace in our resilient pace.

So when the world seems dark and cold,
And the weight of adversity takes its hold,
Remember, within you lies the might,
To turn the darkest storm to light.

In every challenge, in every fall,
Resilience stands, unyielding through it all.
Growth will follow, as sure as the dawn,
In the aftermath of trials, we are reborn.

Beyond The Noise

In quiet moments, I unearth my core,
Where echoes of old selves no longer soar,
I wander through the silence, not to break,
But to glean wisdom from the stillness I
partake.

No longer driven by words' empty sound,
I find solace where silent truths abound.
Skills are nurtured in the calm of dusk,
Each craft a token of my newfound trust.

Financial support is now my own decree,
An affirmation to the strength that sets me
free.
I react not to the voices of the throng,
In their clamor, I find I no longer belong.

Each day unveils a self more refined,
In the tapestry of growth, my soul aligned.
No more a prisoner to past's faint call,
I embrace the quiet, where I find my all.

Thus, in the peace of self I've come to know,
A journey of silence, where my true self
grows.
In the stillness, I am reborn anew,
A better version, steadfast and true.

Encounter With My Soul

In the sanctum of stillness, where the mind
takes flight,
Amidst the shadows of thought, in the depth
of night,
I met a presence, profound and pure,
A soul entwined with mine, an essence
obscure.

In meditation's quiet, where words lose their
way,
I found a whisper, in the silence it lay,
Not a voice, but a feeling, ancient and deep,
A silent communion, where the heart dares to
leap.

The soul revealed itself, not in light, but in
grace,
In a space where the self leaves no trace,
A dance of energies, a celestial embrace,
Beyond the realm of time and place.

No language could capture the depth of this
sight,
A connection so vast, so boundless in might,
In that speechless moment, truth was
unsealed,
A bond so sacred, no words could reveal.

It was not in the talking, but in the silent
breath,
Where the soul spoke truths beyond life and
death,
In the sacred silence, my spirit took flight,
Finding its mirror in the infinite night.

In the echo of the void, I found my own song,
A melody of being, where I truly belong,
In the presence of my soul, where all was laid
bare,
Speechless, I listened, with a heart laid bare.

An Ode To What Sustains

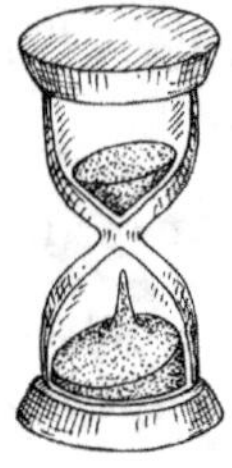

Gratitude swells within me for the quiet ally,
For the coins and notes that pass through my
hands,
Steady and constant, funding the life I live,
Enabling dreams to unfurl in the daylight.

You, the silent provider,
Transforming labor into comfort,
Translating effort into moments of joy,
For me and those I hold dear.

In your presence, I find the means
To build a shelter, warm and secure,
To share a meal with loved ones gathered,
And to weave memories in the fabric of time.

You buy more than just material things—
You purchase peace, the space to breathe,
The freedom to choose and to give,

A life that reflects the values I cherish.
So, I thank you, not as a master,
But as a tool, a trusted companion,
That helps craft a life of happiness,
For me and for those who walk this path with
me.

The Voice Of The Voiceless

I raise up my voice, not in tempestuous roar,
But to be a beacon where silence implores.
Not to echo my own, but to break the dark
hush,
And give sound to the whispers that yearn to
rush.

In the shadows where stories remain untold,
I speak for the hearts that are silent and cold.
Their voices are lost in the clamor of might,
I bring forth their truths to illuminate the
night.

My words are not for my own gain or pride,
But to lift up the ones who in silence abide.
For in their quiet, there lies a plea,
And I am the vessel to set their voices free.

Let the strength of my utterance be their
embrace,
To carry their struggles with dignity and
grace.
In my cadence, may their dreams take flight,
And in their quiet, find their voice's light.

So I raise up my voice with purpose and care,
To echo the unheard, their stories declare.
For in giving them sound, my own soul finds
peace,
As the chorus of the voiceless begins its
release.

Breaking The Chains Within

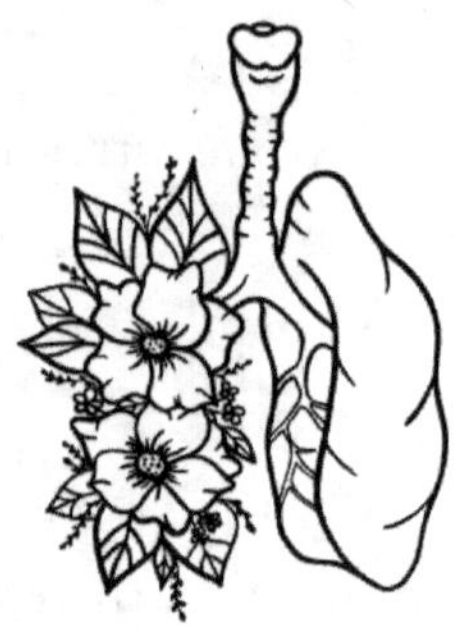

In a world where voices often dictate the way,
I found myself lost, just drifting with the
sway.
Bound by rules I never truly made,
Chasing dreams in a never-ending parade.

Society's whispers, carved my path,
But deep inside, there simmered a silent
wrath.
A need to break free, to rise above the noise,
To find my own rhythm, to make my own
choice.

No longer a prisoner to others' demands,
I tore off the labels with my own hands.
No more seeking approval, no more need to
please,
I chose to live life on my own terms, at ease.

Now, liberation is the air I breathe,
With every step, I let my soul seethe.
From the chains of expectation, I'm finally
free,
In this newfound space, I've discovered the
real me.

The Unbroken Line Of Strength

In this house, where wisdom finds its roots,
Three generations of women have stood,
Each a pillar, steadfast and unyielding,
Not to the winds of time, nor the storms of
fate.

The first, a pioneer in a world unknown,
Carved her path with hands uncalloused, yet
firm.
She bore the weight of expectations unmet,
Yet did not falter, nor let her spirit bow.

Her daughter, no less a force of will,
Took the torch with grace, and in her stride,
Balanced the scales of ambition with nurture,
Her shadow long, her legacy etched in stone.

And now, I stand, the third in this line,
Carrying not just their name, but their fire.
In my veins runs the strength of battles
fought,
In my heart, the echoes of their voices, clear
and true.

The children watch, their eyes wide with
wonder,
Seeing not just the women we are,
But the warriors we became,
In a world that often tried to silence our roar.

They will learn, as I have learned,
That strength is not in muscle, but in mind,
And that to be a woman is not a role,
But a destiny, written in the stars above.

And so, the legacy flows, like a river
unbroken,
From grandmother to mother, now to me.
A chain of empowerment, unsevered by time,
Guiding the next, as we were guided before.

The Waning Hearth

In the quiet of these hollow halls,
I search for echoes of a home once mine,
Where burdens fell like autumn leaves,
And every corner held a gentle sigh.

There was a time, so long ago,
When walls embraced with warmth and care,
And the world outside could not intrude
Upon the solace found within.

Now I dwell in rooms unknown,
Where faces change with passing days,
And voices, kind yet not the same,
Speak words that do not touch the heart.

My children, scattered to distant shores,
Build lives where I am but a name,
And the love I once knew so well
Now lingers only in the past.

My wife, my dear, she left too soon,
Her absence sharp, a constant ache,
And I am left to wander here,
A stranger in a borrowed space.

But in my mind, I close my eyes,
And find the hearth that once was bright,
Where every corner whispered home,
And I, unburdened, found my peace.

Memories Of The Forgotten Self

In the stillness of my soul,
Where the world's clamor fades to whispers,
I trace the outlines of a past
That lingers like the scent of autumn leaves,
Fading yet ever present.

Memories dance like ghosts in the twilight,
Neither fully seen nor truly gone,
They hold the weight of what was,
And the sorrow of what can never be again.

A life once vibrant with the colors of youth,
Now softened to shades of grey,
It rests within me, not as a burden,
But as a tender reminder of the paths I've
walked.

In these quiet moments, I feel the pull,
A yearning for a time untouched by the harsh
hands of reality,
Yet I remain here, in the now,
Carrying with me the echoes of a self
That shaped the person I have become.

Not lost, but transformed,
The past lives within me,
A silent companion in the journey forward,
Its reverence felt in every beat of my heart.

The Source Within

If you wander the world seeking love,
Do not chase its fleeting forms,
The tender hands, the longing eyes,
Or the whispered promises under a quiet sky.

For love, true love, is not a thing to be found
In another's embrace or in the corners of a
smile.
It resides within, deep in the marrow,
In the pulse of your own being.

The heart is not just a vessel to be filled
By another's affection,
But a source, a wellspring,
Overflowing with the capacity to give.

Seek not the beloved in another's gaze,
But in the quiet corners of your own soul,
Where love rises, unbidden,
A boundless river, ever-flowing.

In the search for love,
Turn inward, where the source lies still,
And there, you will meet the beloved,
Not as a stranger, but as a reflection of
yourself.

The Echo Of Listening

I thank the gift, this silent grace,
To hold my words, let them rest untouched.
To step away from the noise,
To make space for the echoes of others.
To be the quiet shore,
Where restless waves come to break and find
peace,
To be the stillness,
That cradles what is said, what is felt,
unspoken.
There is a beauty in restraint,
In choosing not to fill the air
When the world spills over
With its untamed clamor, its urgent pleas.

Listening is an act of love,
A patience that does not seek a spotlight.
It is in this listening,
I find the depth, the resonance
Of being part of all that is spoken
And all that finds rest in the spaces between.
In the stillness, I hear the truths
That words cannot contain or express.
It is here, within the quiet,
That hearts speak their sincerest messages.
And as I sit with the silence,
I discover a strength that is not loud or
bright—
But a quiet power,
A gentle force that anchors, heals, and holds.

The Quiet Gift Of Forgiveness

It lies within, unseen and still,
A quiet gift wrapped in tenderness,
Not in words spoken, nor deeds confessed,
But in the gentle unbinding of the heart.

It lifts the weight of time's old scars,
Softly unravels the knots of grief,
Not with triumph, nor with shouts,
But with a silent yielding to release.

It does not seek to mend the past,
Nor paint over wounds long healed,
It simply opens the door of the soul,
And lets the light pour in, unhindered.

Forgiveness breathes where blame once
dwelled,
And fills the spaces left by hurt,
It does not ask for pardon or praise,
Only to dissolve, quietly, into peace.

A Hollow Calm That Stills My Heart

A numbness strange that haunts my weary
soul,
No joy doth sing, no sorrow stirs within,
The heart beats faint, yet lacks a fervent goal,
As if in dreams where life and breath grow
thin.

No tears do fall, nor laughter graces speech,
A hollow calm pervades this vacant breast,
Emotions once so bold, now out of reach,
And passion's flame lies smothered into rest.

What spell hath stilled the fire in my veins?
What cruel enchantment steals my spirit's
cry?
For even pain, that friend of honest pains,
Now passeth by with cold and distant eye.

Perchance, in time, the winds of life shall
blow,
And stir again what slumbers deep below.
Yet still, within this silent, hollow space,
A spark remains, though buried beneath the
snow,
And in the dark, I find a quiet grace,
A whispered hope that one day it shall grow.
For though the storm may hide the stars
above,
The dawn will rise and chase the night away,
And in the light, my heart shall find its love,
Awake once more to dance in life's bright day.
So let the winds of change begin to blow,
And stir again what slumbers deep below.

Between Shadow And Self

It came to me as it comes to all,
Quietly, without warning or fuss,
Like dusk settles on a field,
And night falls without a sound.

There was no cry, no sudden break,
Just the slow fading of light,
The warmth that once found in words
Grew cold, and I did not notice.

I walked the paths I always knew,
But the colors were less bright,
The wind that stirred the leaves
Did not move me the same way.

And so I stood, as others have,
Caught between feeling and void,
Wondering if the world had changed,
Or if it was only me.

But in that hush, I found a seed,
A whisper soft yet deep and clear:
Perhaps in loss, there's space to grow,
A new light waiting to appear.

Untraceable Steps

Some choices are made in silence,
A quiet nod to the unknown—
Not for their wisdom or faultlessness,
But because they waited, patient,
While the only doors stood open.

The world did not halt for pondering,
Nor offer signs to guide in the dark;
We moved forward, knowing there'd be no
hands to hold,
Only the weight of our steps,
Marked softly in the earth behind us.

It is not regret that follows,
But a kind of reverent holding—
Of paths we cannot unwalk,
Of echoes that drift and linger,
As reminders, softly placed.

So we live, as the day demands,
Upright beneath what we've chosen,
Finding, perhaps, a quiet grace
In the courage to remain still,
And to make each step a tribute
To the one before.

The Distance Of Growing Up

In the gentle curve of time,
Our parents wear their years
Not as a cloak of aging,
But as a testament to our flight.

Each day, a feather shed,
As we stretch our wings in solitude.
Once, their hands were the steady ground,
The roots that held us close.

But as we reach for skies anew,
We drift, unanchored, from their warmth,
Turning our backs on quiet comforts,
Leaving them in silence.

Lonely shadows of our former selves.
Their laughter, once a symphony,
Now echoes in the stillness,
And the wisdom shared in tender nights
Fades like a whisper in a crowded room.

Where we now stand,
Illuminated by our own bright flames,
Yet casting them into dusk.
Do they know the weight of this distance?
That in our quest for independence,
We unintentionally weaved a tapestry
Of longing where closeness once thrived?

In their eyes, I see the flicker,
A wish for the past,
A yearning for connection
In the space we've carved with our choices.
As we grow, may we not forget
That love is a thread, ever binding.

Even in the dance of becoming us
We can reach back, extend our hands,
And find the balance of togetherness
In the gentle embrace of growing up.

The Gift Of Intellect

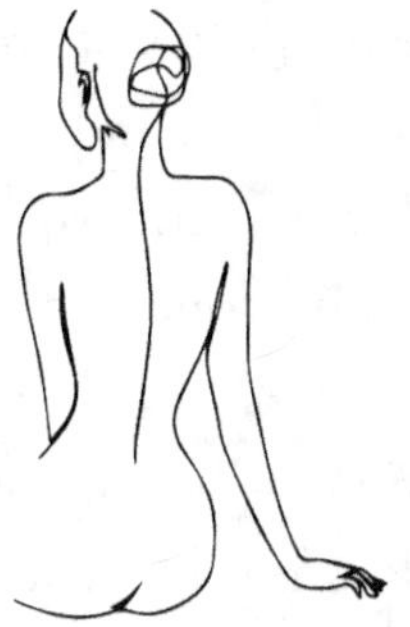

Grateful am I for this spark within,
A silent fire that shapes my being,
A gift not worn on the skin,
But rooted deep, in the fabric of the soul.

To think, to know, to question
These are not mere tools,
But the breath of life itself,
The compass that points to purpose
And the path of understanding.

While others wander through the haze,
Moved by instincts, shadows of knowledge,
I stand upon the mountain's edge,
Seeing the world with open eyes
And the weight of wisdom in my hands.

This intellect, both fragile and fierce,
Is a bridge that links me
To the mysteries of creation,
To the hum of stars and endless skies,
To the silent truths,
Hidden in stone and stream.

For in thought lies my humanity,
A fire that does not burn yet illuminates,
That does not conquer but reveals,
Drawing me closer to the essence of life,
Where the mind bows to the spirit,
And the self meets the eternal.

The Pillar Of Character

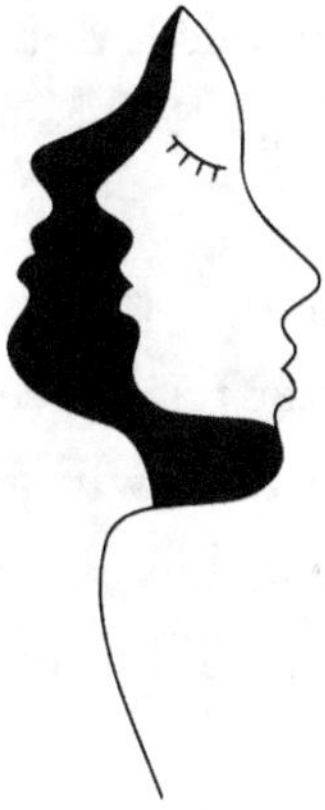

There lies no power so lasting,
Nor influence so quietly profound,
As the steady hand of reputation,
Not wrought of wealth or idle praise,
But by the steady pulse of integrity's heart.

A life well-lived becomes its own defense,
A monument rising firm and tall
Against the fickle tides of fortune,
Against the passing winds of envy and scorn.
True reputation seeks no trumpet's call.

No gilded cloak nor boasting cry;
It grows in silent, patient hours,
In faithful deeds done unseen,
And in kindness bestowed, unasked.

For it is in character that strength resides,
In the quiet resilience of truth,
In bearing burdens with upright grace,
While the world looks on, uncertain,
And finds itself humbled, stilled.

Let reputation be the pillar, the unmoving
stone,
Not adorned by fleeting words,
But carved through trials faced with honor,
And made unassailable, enduring,
A fortress in the soul of all that is just.

In The Space Between Words

Speak gently, for the universe leans close,
Each word a pebble cast in silent waters,
Rippling far beyond our fleeting knowing,
To touch shores unseen and souls
unmeasured.

There is power in a word withheld,
A strength in silence, softly kept,
A grace in speaking less than need
For truth needs neither flourish nor sound.

Grateful, then, be for each breath,
For the syllables shaped in quiet awe,
As if the stars themselves would gather
To hear the whispers of a single heart.

And in that hush, that space of stillness,
Feel the weight and wonder held within,
Knowing each word may plant a seed—
A quiet offering, left for eternity.

www.ingramcontent.com/pod-product-compliance
Lightning Source LLC
LaVergne TN
LVHW011054200726
843509LV00011B/1407